THE FOUR NOBLE TRUTHS

DUKKHA
SAMUDAYA
MAGGA
NIRODHA

Illustrated By
Ayan Saha

Dharma Wisdom, LLC

Written by
Christine H. Huynh, M.D.

The Four Noble Truths

Bringing the Buddha's Teachings into Practice series

Copyright © 2023 by Dharma Wisdom, LLC

All rights reserved.

Published in the United States of America by Dharma Wisdom, LLC. No part of this book may be reproduced or transmitted in any form or by any means, electronic or mechanical, including photocopying, recording, or by any information storage and retrieval system without the prior written permission of the author, except for the inclusion of brief quotations in critical reviews and certain other noncommercial uses permitted by copyright law. For permission requests or information, please contact the publisher.

Dharma Wisdom, LLC
Arlington, Texas
dharmawisdomdw@gmail.com

Author: Christine H. Huynh, M.D.
Illustrator: Ayan Saha

Library of Congress
Control Number: 2023913313

ISBN: 978-1-951175-19-1

First Edition 2023

There are different truths in life.
The absolute or relative truths should not
  cause any strife.
The relative truth is based on our perception.
The absolute is true without any question.

With the relative truth, we see a chair.
It could be made of wood and nails,
   we may be unaware.
The truth is that the sun is hot.
This is absolute, whether we believe it or not.

The sun is absolutely hot!

Life is balanced with pairs of opposites.
Happiness and sadness are two correlates.
One cannot exist without the other.
We only want the positives, and nothing further.

We also have personal truths.
The body's aging and sickness are proof
Along with our seven emotions
    that fluctuate.
They are objects of mindfulness
    for us to meditate.

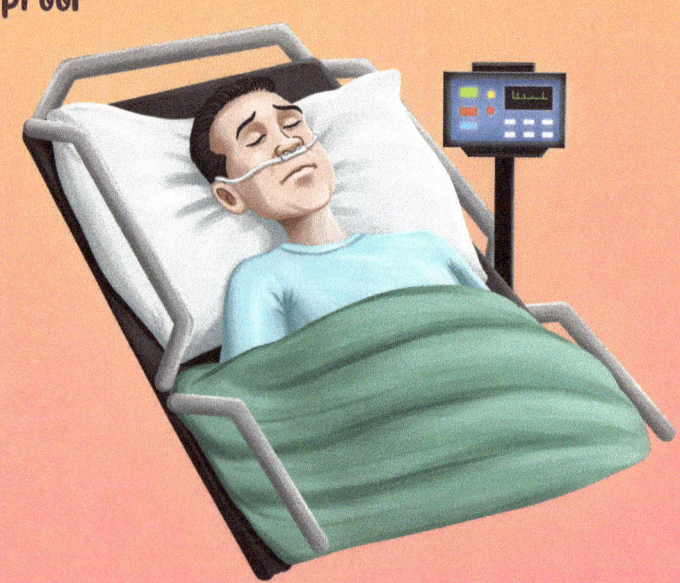

Joy, anger, happiness, sadness,
Love, hate, and cravings are objects for our practice.
Joy, happiness, and love are great.
They are positive feelings for us to celebrate.

The Buddha is the great physician
Who can see all of our addictions.
He proclaimed the Four Noble Truths
Similar to a physician's thoughts and attributes.

Symptoms, diagnosis, prognosis, and therapy
Are the steps to treat illnesses of the mind and body.
Dukkha, samudaya, nirodha, and *magga*
Are the Buddha's Four Truths to transform our karma.

DUKKHA

Pain Ill-being

Dissatisfaction

The first truth, *dukkha*, points out pain and ill-being.
We should try to understand them with total knowing.
Look deeply to see our dissatisfaction
When we do not get what we want, *dukkha* happens.

SAMUDAYA

The second truth, *samudaya*, explains the cause of *dukkha*
The path that gives rise to all the drama.
Find out what it is so we can let go.
It is our craving and clinging we must outgrow.

NIRODHA

Well-being

Liberation

The third truth, *nirodha*, declares the end of *dukkha*.
Realize that there is a way to nirvana.
The ceasing of ill-being results in well-being.
Liberation is what we will be seeing.

MAGGA

The fourth truth, *magga*, shows us the path to follow.
The Noble Eightfold Path should be our motto:
Develop right view, thought, speech, and actions
Right livelihood, effort, mindfulness, and concentration.

Dukkha occurs when we have pain in our teeth.
This feeling alerts us of a problem, indeed.
Finding the cause is the next step we should take.
Craving for sweets and not brushing are our mistakes.

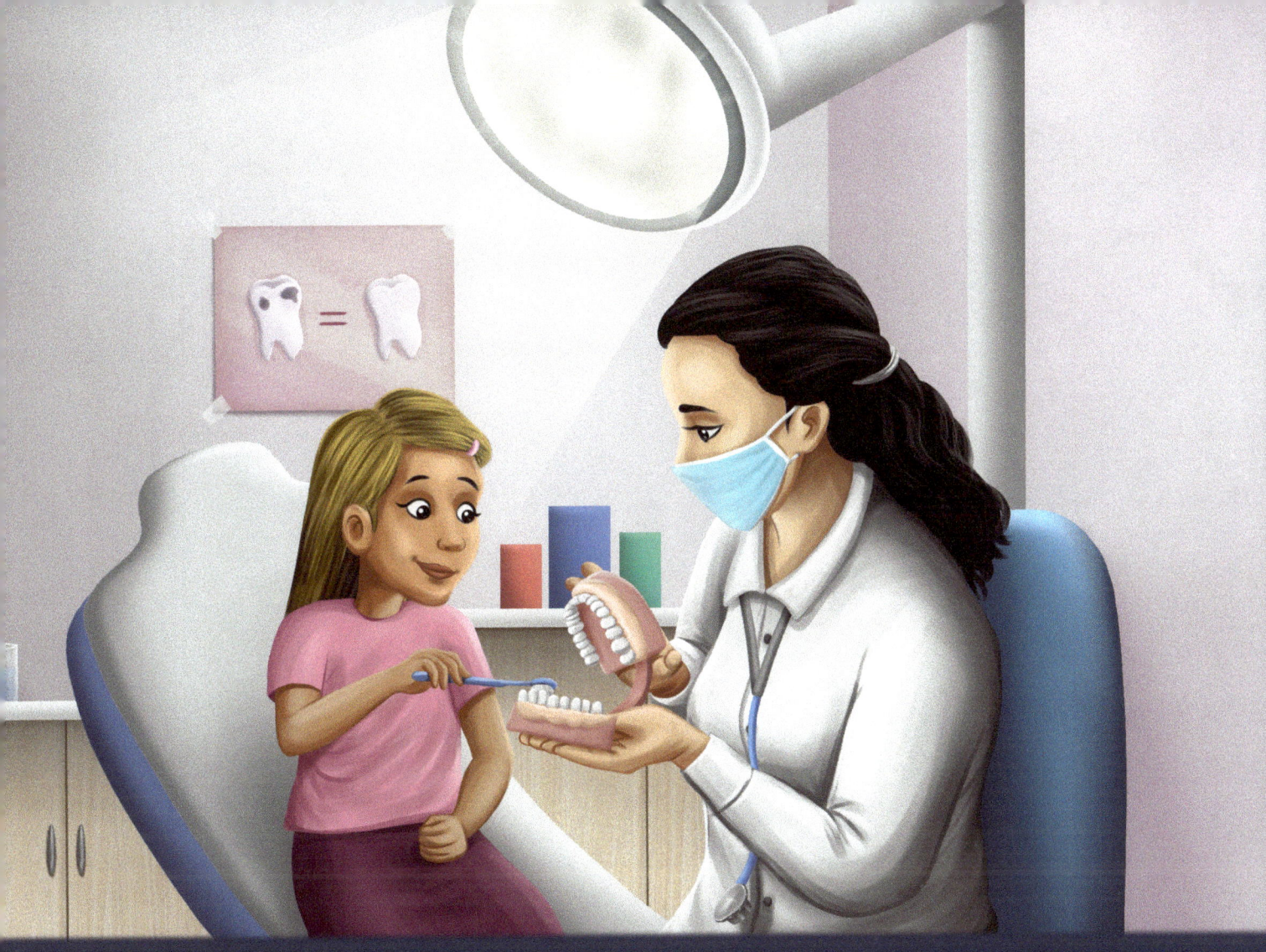

The teeth doctor states there's a way to get better
To be free from pain and all the fetters.
We should focus to develop correct views and thoughts.
Be mindful and tell ourselves to diligently brush and floss.

Dukkha appears when we are angry
Because anger causes us to suffer badly
When we are far from people whom we love
Or being close to those with whom we've had enough.

Look within and find out why anger is present
To find out the arising cause that is unpleasant.
It may be craving for things we cannot have
Or clinging onto things that are gone in a flash.

When there is a beginning, there is an ending.
Anger fades away after some mending.
Its cessation leads to happiness and joy.
See it for yourself, it is not a ploy.

Follow the Noble Eightfold Path without hesitation.
Practice skillful views, thoughts, speech, and actions.

Live in the present moment and enjoy our blessings.
Offer compassion and understanding in any setting.

Practice diligently, focus and see.
Don't water the seed of anger, let it be.
Recognize it and allow it to subside.
These are the skills to gain deep insight.

The Four Noble Truths is a core principle teaching.
After his Enlightenment, the Buddha said in his preaching
In the First Sermon at Sarnath to his five ascetic friends.
He set the Dharma Wheel in motion so we can comprehend.

8 spoked Dharma wheel

12 spoked Dharma wheel

The Dharma Wheel that has eight spokes
Portrays the Eightfold Path for us to note.
The twelve-spoked Dharma Wheel defines
Turning the Four Noble Truths in motion three times.

In the first turning of the wheel the Buddha revealed
The Four Noble Truths is declared with a seal.

In the second turning of the wheel the Buddha realized
Dukkha is overcome with the Eightfold Path as a guide.

In the third turning of the wheel the Buddha asserted
We, too, can achieve liberation and enlightenment as expected.
By undertaking the Four Noble Truths and practicing the Eightfold Path
Our well-being, joy, and merits will amass.

The Dharma Wheel is round and is easily rolled.
Wherever it rolls, it strikes out pain and suffering manifold.

It helps us cross from this shore to the other shore.
With this profound teaching we will soar.

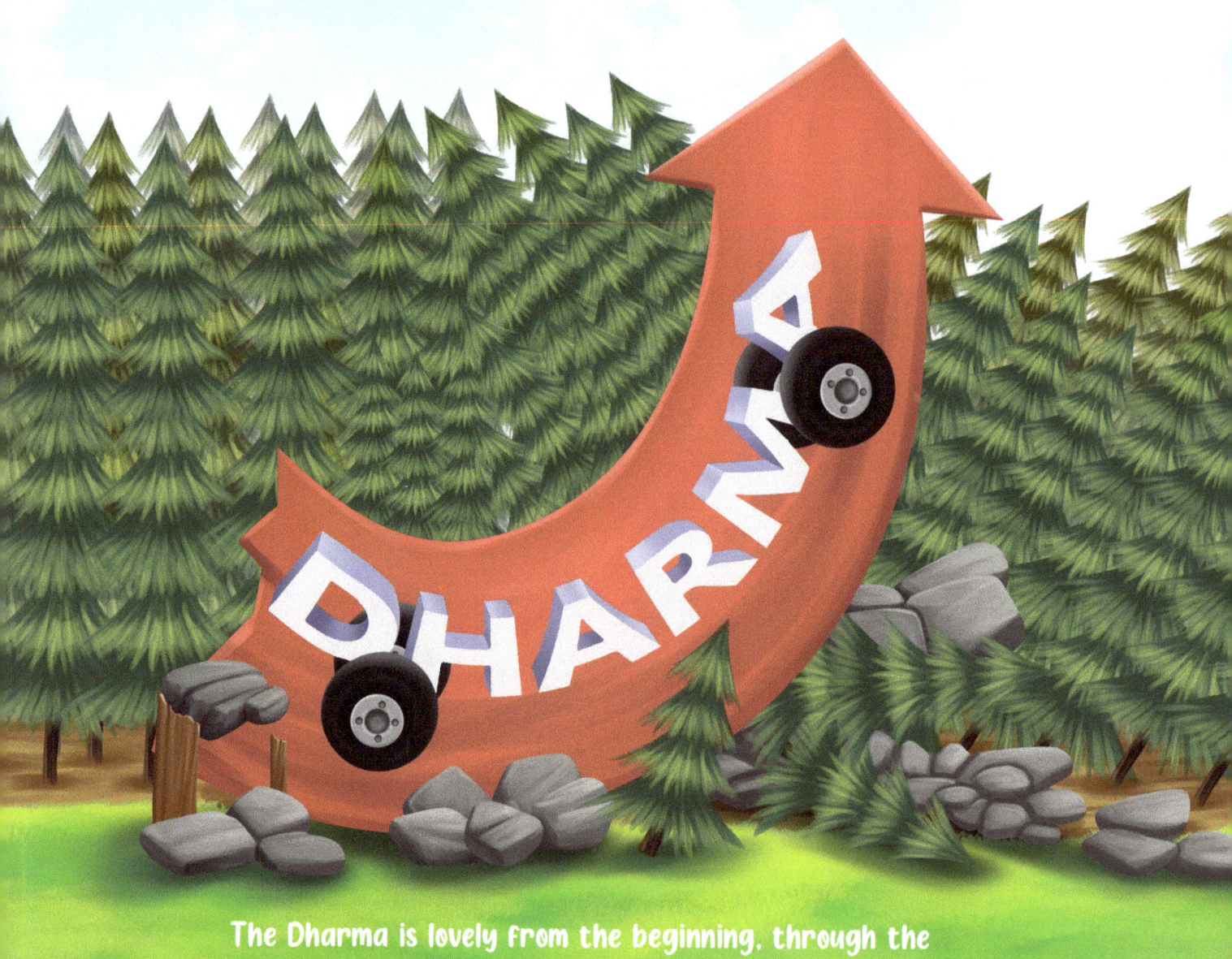

The Dharma is lovely from the beginning, through the middle and end.
It picks up what has fallen and straightens out any bend.
It directs us in the right path when we are lost.
It shines in a place of darkness to bring out a gloss.

DHARMA

The Dharma is clear and visible, present at all times.
It invites and uplifts us now and beyond our prime.
The Buddha's teaching is like a lion's roar
Reaching the beginner's mind and the hardcore.

Dharma practice makes us anew.
Studying without practice leads to false views.
Practice without studying results in misunderstanding.
Mindfully listen, reflect, and practice with all abiding.

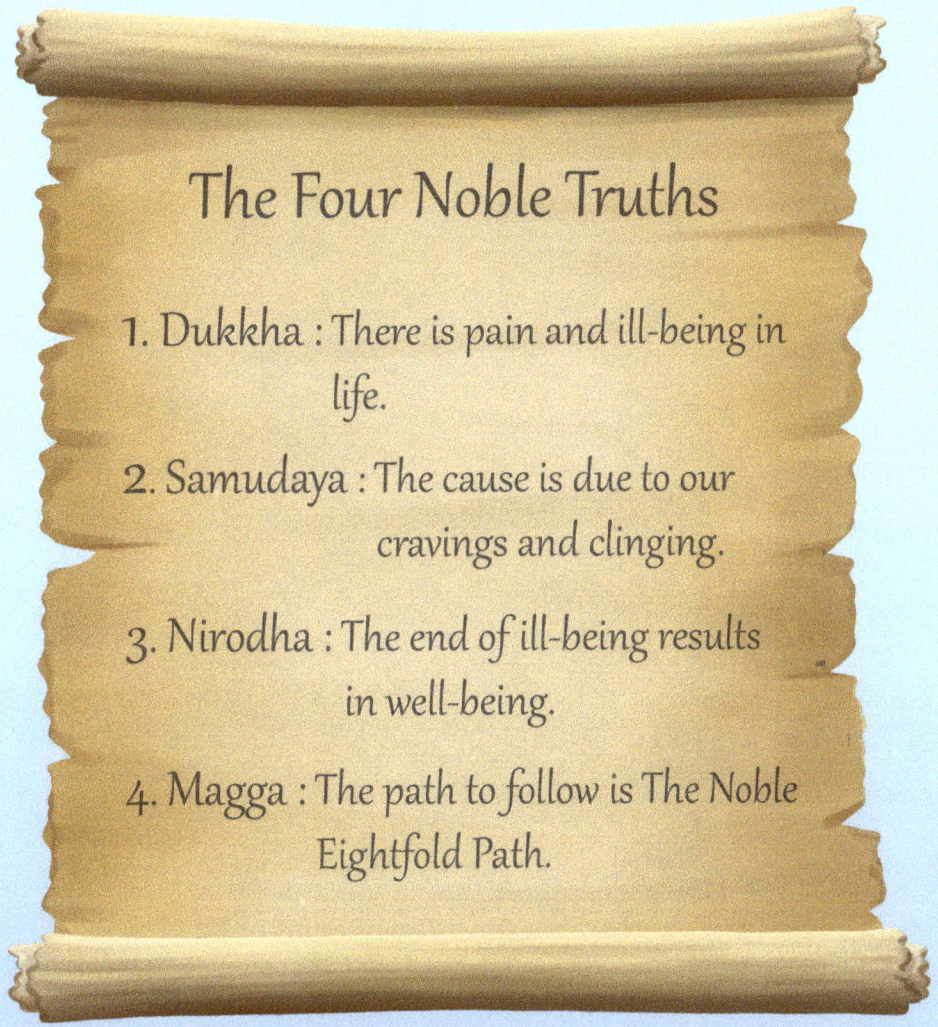

Countless prayers for all living beings to be liberated.
And their immeasurable sufferings to be totally eradicated.
Let's commit to study and practice the Dharma teachings
So we all can achieve the supreme path of awakening.

The Four Noble Truths is noble because
It has the power to liberate all of us.
These four tasks serve as objects of our cultivation
For us to attain awakening and perfect wisdom.

www.ingramcontent.com/pod-product-compliance
Lightning Source LLC
Chambersburg PA
CBHW051403110526
44592CB00023B/2934